The Hallelujah Series
and Other Poems

Also by Arthur J. Stewart

Rough Ascension and Other Poems of Science

Bushido: The Virtues of Rei and Makoto

Circle, Turtle, Ashes

The Ghost in the Word

From Where We Came

Elements of Chance

The Hallelujah Series
and Other Poems

by Arthur J. Stewart

Periploi Press
NASHVILLE, TENNESSEE
2021

Copyright © 2021
First edition

All rights reserved. No part of this publication may be reproduced, stored in a retrieval system, or transmitted in any form or by any means—electrical, photocopy, recording, or others—except for brief quotations in written reviews, without the prior written permission of the publisher.

Design by Dariel Mayer

Manufactured in the United States of America

ISBN: 978-0-9830115-8-3
Library of Congress Control Number: 2021908563

For my sister Bonnie

~

*an amazing artist
and a beautiful person.*

Contents

Preface and Acknowledgments   ix

Part 1

Pathway	3
When I Say Alleluia	4
The Hallelujah Series	5
Changing Lanes	10
Gone, the Prescient Dreams	14
At a Soup's-On Fundraising Event	15
Adrift	16
As If	17
Again and Again	18
Message	20
On a Recruiting Trip to Niagara Falls	21
Pure Gold	22
Learning through Travel	24
Back to Edges	30
Starting the Thing	31
In the Shade	32
I Lost It, Archie	33
Peeper Frogs in Early March	35
Screaming in a Dream	36
Some Things Pretend	37
Stasis	38
What's Left	40
The Last	41

Part 2

Strange Light	45
A Slug While Hiking in Basque Country	46
Ambition	47
Waiting for Inspiration	48
By Satellite and Magazine	50
Teaching a Science-Writing Workshop	51
With the Margarita Half Gone	52
Fukushima Boars	53
This Is for All the Forgetting	54
Learning to Fly	55
Timing Is Everything	56
Structure	57
The Rough Side of Spring	58
Demise of the Waggle Dance	60
On Making a Tuna Salad Sandwich	61
Blank Page	62
A Small Hibernaculum, Revisited	63
No Hallelujahs	65
I Feel So Earthy and Down at Home	67
Not Today, It Doesn't	68
Not the Same	70

About the Author   71

Preface and Acknowledgments

For the last several decades, my overarching objective has been to show how science and poetry complement one another and how these two great human constructs stem from the same motherlode of intellectual curiosity about who we are, why we are here, and how things work. The poems in this book, *The Hallelujah Series and Other Poems*, continue that effort, with a focus on place.

From responses to my earlier works, I learned that many scientists enjoy science-themed poems, but most do not know quite what to make of poetry, scientifically themed or not. Further, many readers with a more literary background seem only marginally interested in scientific details. From these observations, I conclude that C. P. Snow's paradigm[1] about the two cultures is still firm, despite efforts to make the science-poetry boundary more transparent and permeable.

In this collection, most of the poems touch only lightly on things firmly in the science domain, for two reasons. First, my days as an active scientist are now largely over. While I still enjoy reading and learning about science, and teaching science, I'm reasonably well past the doing-science phase of my life. The business of living now has taken precedence, and my writing tendencies have directed themselves accordingly. Second, having tried with limited success to lure scientists into more literary ways of thinking about their scientific works through poetry, I thought it might be good to see if I could entice more literary-focused readers to consider venturing deeper into science.

Global climate change is now knocking hard on the door, and we need everyone possible to begin changing things for the better, very quickly. Else, I fear, we'll leave a serious mess to our children and our children's children. So, comfortable or not, scientific experts and specialists in the literary arts must find ways to communicate effectively with each other across C. P. Snow's so-called cultural divide. We need scientists with heart and strong communication skills, and we need literary artists with a deep, appreciative understanding of science.[2] These two pools of expertise absolutely must unite under a strong sense of place—Earth, our island home. Further, I remain confident that poetry can serve effectively as a commons area for accomplishing this task.

Words, metaphors, similes, and images—these things remain valuable tools for persuasion and developing a shared vision, and we need to be facile with these tools to begin changing ourselves and our behaviors in ways that might allow a more sustainable existence on Earth. So, in considering these points, where are we, individually, with respect to place? Where are we with respect to our thinking, our feelings, our very existence, spatially and temporally? What is next to us, and what, truth said, is far away?

The works of two poets, William Carlos Williams (1883–1963) and Archie Ammons (1926–2001), particularly intrigue me in thinking about place. Williams was a family physician and pediatrician and was wonderfully observant of the natural world; Ammons was (in part) a "nature poet," which requires strong observational skills of the external world and of the self. Ammons also developed a unique writing style, conspicuously evident in what I view to be some of his best works, *Garbage* and *Glare*. So, several poems in this collection allude to works by Williams and Ammons. In particular, with respect to place, long live Archie Ammons' "Easter Morning"!

Two poems in this collection—Pathway and Blank Page—are included with permission in *Becoming a Teacher Who Writes: Let Teaching Be Your Writing Muse*. (Gorrell, N. (2021). Equinox. Sheffield, UK and Oakville, CT).

Special thanks to Robert Louis Chianese for his astute comments, and to Linda Parsons for her editorial skills and sensitivities: together, they helped make this collection better. And special thanks to Jim Johnston: his poetry analysis skills are superb.

---

1. Snow, C. P. *The Two Cultures*. New York: Cambridge University Press, 1969.
2. Edward O. Wilson, in dialog with former U.S. Poet Laureate Robert Hass, noted that "the ideal scientist thinks like a poet and works like a bookkeeper." 2012.

PART 1

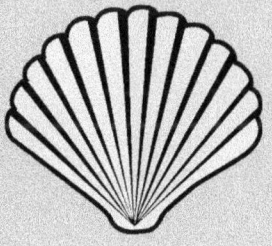

Pathway

Years ago, when I first
readied myself to set out
into the world, I had a vivid dream

about ploughing a field,
with red soil on one side and white soil
on the other. The plough

was rough and made of wood and it cast
red soil onto the white soil, and white soil
onto the red soil and for years that image held,
sometimes cloudy and sometimes clear.

I worked thereafter
to make it so: mixing
science and poetry, two strong modes
of creativity, two ways

for understanding the world.

Hallelujah, I say,
looking forward, living the dream
or dreaming
while living—

when I have filled
that which I can fill,
it is done.

It is over.

When I Say Alleluia

several times in succession, it sounds false
    or outdated: it is a word
that came into being perhaps

thousands of years ago
when causal things were not well
understood, thousands of years ago

when a mysterious higher-order sense of
responsible actions
made more sense. For what are we searching

now, when we say the word?
Praise be, yes—but does it also mean
a greater giving up of fact, or a greater

acceptance of things we'd rather not
think too hard about, for fear
of finding something

more glorious, or more banal,
holding things up?
Well, the word has spawned

so many songs, great swaths
of music: imagine
waves of praise all ye, Yah,

rising, hill after distant hill, ascending
in a massive chorus, an offering
to flowers, fields, mountains.

I can say the word honestly
each day, thanks for the previous day,
when the sun cracks pink over the eastern ridge.

The Hallelujah Series

1 ■
Hallelujah! The word comes
to my way of thinking
before the thing, in heralding mode, expressing
awe and appreciation
for the wonderful thing coming, whereas

alleluia comes after,
signifying thanks, for the wonderful thing done.
Brackets, in short,
for wonder and appreciation, left and right,
for good things: mainly a difference

in tense, or temporal perspective. I'm sure
biblical scholars will challenge that.

2 ■
The mitral valve in the heart
permits a one-way flow of blood:
a back-flow preventer, the one,
in my mom, that's not working: it leaks
like a sieve
and it's getting worse. Morphine
takes care of the symptoms, a little—my sister gives it
when the heart begins racing,
and the body struggles,

trying to keep the body alive.

It's too late
to get it fixed. She's
93 and her doctor said
if she went under, she'd stay there. Now
the heart races, a stripped gear,

a futile longing to sustain life.
Alleluia.

3 ■
Morning early
I rumble around
with the computer—I check out

earthquakes around the world,
learn what's up
with the H_5N_1 influenza virus,
scout activity of volcanos—Katla
would be a beast and now she's twitchy.

Here and there, I look over
the news and read
interesting scientific advances. But then

it's time to settle down to write
and if
something good comes,
alleluia.

4 ■
I'll not tip
my hand too soon—
but sometimes I can see myself becoming
a little old man:

hunched shoulders, thin white hair,
half-moon
spectacles, the paunch
I hope will go by then but now

only the HVAC sighs and someone
in the Grace Point kitchen fiddles
at making coffee. Strong,
I hope.

The Bunn
appears to be simple enough to operate:
the carafes are stained
and there are written directions.

At last
the brown trickle begins.
It smells great and I say
alleluia for that.

5 ▪

With the coffee half-gone, it's time
to review the world in wonder.
Outside this place, a mist is rising
over the lake;
it softens the light from the houses
on the far shore. It's said God said

"let there be light and there was light"
and God saw
the light was good.

A doe
surely must be stirring
in the woods on the far shore, too.
She might or might not know God.
She raises and turns her head,
looking over the water.
The deer's body
emerges from the mist as a solid thing.

6 ▪

    I loop back to the time
    of the shining black slug in Spain.

    We were pilgrims then,
    hiking

    each day to the fullest,
    vineyards

    sometimes on both sides of us.
    Their vines

    abided in us, and we in them.
    We did not prune them. Nor did He.

    At least, not that we knew of then.
    Day by day now, the barren vines

    are getting clipped.
    The little stubs bleed

    and the old cane will get cast
    into the fire. Have faith,

    old soul, there will be fruit aplenty.

7 ▪

    The sister's voice is tinny
    so far away, over the phone.
    More morphine
    under the tongue
    last night, and with this

    information, time
    twists, shortens, begins to blur.

    I cannot say
    hallelujah or alleluia,
    thanks be to God.

8 ▪

    Jesus said, "My hour has not yet come."
    But his mom
    bypassed his intent and gave orders

    to the servants, saying "Do
    whatever he tells you."

    It does not say
    Jesus sighed, but I'll bet he did
    before doing what his mom wanted:
    and he turned
    water into good wine.
    Alleluia.

Changing Lanes

1 ■
By phone the sister said
we're in the home stretch,
the mom has entered
a new phase.

Sometimes
she makes sense and sometimes not.
Unable
to make it to the bathroom

even with her walker; the last
shreds of dignity fall
to the floor. It is March,
so I could say

there're just a few seconds left
on the shot-clock,
not enough time
for a game-tying three.

I take a breath and think
Circle, Turtle, Ashes.
Deep sorrow, hallelujah.

2 ■
Each workday I do two
death-defying things.
First, when coming home I merge
off Solway Road onto Pellissippi Parkway.

Cars there, at that time of day, are
shoulder to shoulder, going too fast.
I take a deep breath, flick on
the blinker, accelerate

like crazy and hope.

And hope.

The second action
is something like the first—I merge
from Lovell Road onto US 75/40.
Trucks, big bastards, 18-wheelers, fill
the two lanes on the right, they're all going

75 or so, huffing hard as they carry things
through Knoxville to Chattanooga
or on to Nashville or farther west, some
perhaps as far as Phoenix and

to merge I take a breath, match speed and thread
tight between two trucks and wait
for chance to pass
faster in the left-hand lane. Mornings
are less dicey; the traffic is thinner then.

3 ■

So threading back to the sister,
to the hallelujah time, to morning, to she
who gave and gives

graciously of herself to the mom's care
through that time of
doldrums and declination, into and through
the one-way door

from life
to something else
we will each pass through
on our own terms.

It is

almost the sister's birthday; we're nearing Easter, she's
one year younger, a hundred years
wiser, a thousand years
of love, and outside, being March,

hyacinths, crocuses, daffodils, and
ambiguously, Rose of Sharon rise up
testing life again
despite the recent flood and despite
the earlier intermittent
bouts of cold and warm.

4
Cold and warm.

We seem bound
by our physicality to destroy
things we say we love. We will
ourselves forward through time,
bleak or sometimes glad and yet
in gladness, too, we fall far short.

A delicate web
astonishes us with dew and how it arcs
from gravity and how it bends in breeze;
astounds us
with its chemical simplicity,
its structural form and by the fact it was
pinned in darkness overnight.

All night the garden spider works
around the spokes securing
one line to another, tugging here
and pulling this thread snug to that,
and like that, we too are left
planning but not knowing
if we'll live another day.

Gone, the Prescient Dreams

In a dream, I stoop at the edge of a stream,
reach down and pull up a handful of mud
    and I squeeze
the mud through the fingers, until there,
left behind in the palm of the right hand,
is a nugget of gold.

Now, sixty years looking back, I can see
that dream was prescient: I have worked squeezing
good ecological data from streams
and I have gained much
satisfaction from the small gold

nuggets of good poems
squeezed from the everyday
beauty of science and water.

My dreams no longer seem prescient.
Last night, for example, I dreamed
I was teaching a large group
of graduate students who had arranged themselves
around a long table outdoors, and some
were so far away they could not hear me
even when I spoke loudly. And I was
disappointed because

they didn't much care. And when the class
was over I gathered my things
and by force of will alone I floated
several inches above the ground

and by force of will alone I moved
forward, floating
across campus to an office I had not seen before.

At a Soup's-On Fundraising Event

In my chair, at the Soup's-On fundraising event—
I discover I have become
just another old man: lines and wrinkles,
thinning hair. I lean back a notch and study
the faces of other old men
at the table. I take a sip
of sausage-and-potato soup
using a white plastic spoon. I gnaw
a slice of good buttered bread and watch
for any tremble
of fingers, theirs or mine. Yes,
for the gentleman across the table from me
and no, not yet at least, for mine. I do not know
his name, but he looks

dour, due to a slight
natural downturn at the corners
of his mouth. The gentleman
on his left is more active:
he attacks his soup forcefully.
It is Tuscan chicken. He complains:
the chili was gone. Probably
he would have liked it,
it had more kick
than the soup he sucks down now.

To see his hair in detail I have to raise
my gaze to peer
through the lower part of my glasses.
The hearing aid
stuck deep in my right ear squeals, having picked up
some frequency it amplified
with a vengeance. At my age

things don't work
the way they used to.

Adrift

My memories of her float,
bobbing and dipping

like driftwood adrift
on swells in a large lake.

Sometimes some are in sight
and sometimes they are in-

visible. Not driftwood,
yet like driftwood.

Most of the pieces float
like icebergs—their wet black backs

show above water,
but most of their mass is below, because

the pieces are waterlogged, saturated
to the core. Most of the pieces are wave-

washed to satin smooth. When a piece
at last gets cast to shore by waves, it sun-dries

on sand at the high-water line,
sharing space with the silvery dried

bodies of alewife and the occasional
larger bodied carp. The pieces reveal themselves then

as tree-bones: hard gnarled gray
historical records of time. My fingers

slip over the smooth knobby knots,
the rounded nubs of scars, almost reading.

As If

When I let the thoughts slide
back in time I discover their edges have blurred,
their contents have become
new things, not

better, not
worse. We played chess
and usually she won. The first time
I was on the verge of beating her

she bumped the board, by accident
she said, knocking over
too many pieces to finish the game—
she was that

competitive. She taught me
vanishing-point perspective,
and how to cook, iron and sew, claiming
each child should know these things

as civilized survival skills. Do your best
in school. Call
for help if you really need it.
Get the big picture and attend

to details as if
your life depends on it.

Again and Again

I got up this morning and
after showering said
to myself, this is what I need to do
today: get coffee and
start the dishwasher and
let the dog out and

and and and and and

the day rolls off on some
trajectory and
by noon it's time to start
planning dinner and

when evening settles in at last
we find ourselves

sitting quietly by the koi pond,
sipping margaritas; the waterfall
making perfect sounds, a frog
now and then offering his

intermittent banjo-plucking call and
we swat the occasional mosquito and

although the mom tidied things up
at the end there're still all these
driftwood pieces bobbing, left over
from her death—

I throw the dog's toy
as far as I can over the koi pond and
into the back yard and
Jessie, the dog, runs and

finds it, brings it back all slobbered up and
she wants it thrown again,
and again.

Message

This little message
in a tight-corked bottle

made lavender by age
I cast out for someone

years from now to find.
I am on my way out. The one

who finds this message
may be concerned

with things in their life.
If they are too young

to be married, let him or her find hope,
opportunity, and love.

If in midlife, let them find hope,
opportunity, and love.

And if they, like me, are nearing an end
let them find peace and satisfaction.

On a Recruiting Trip to Niagara Falls

After talking to students for hours
about internships, my voice begins going:
it becomes raspy, the voice of another person,
content less censored,
and sometimes
in frustration I chastise a student
for demonstrating insufficient force or intent—
yes, using my straight gaze,
I tell them

such decisions
should be made with firm intent, not just
that wussy way, like
I'm looking for a summer job.

In the hotel room that night
I am exhausted, having slept
not enough on the plane and

weary now to the bone—weary
to the core, everything is running
together and I try to think

hard about the center of
why we do what we do
and yet
in my sleep that night
I am resurrected
again to the beautiful
chaos of science.

Pure Gold

Emerging
cool in a spring morning, light creeps
first among higher leaves on trees but
soon on grass blades: tiny packets of
energy from the sun, our far-off hard-
working star, fusing and fussing,

busy slamming
molecules positioned
    just so
in leaf-based photo-
reaction centers, packaged

politely (yes, sir!) in

membrane-bound layers like lawyers—
eager beavers without top hats: stacked
like flapjacks, flat surfaces
orienting perpendicularly to the in-
coming stream and

wow! Things start happening,

electrons begin flying around
like energetic baseballs, get snagged,
roll energy
into wads of
green banknotes shoved

into deep pockets, signed, sealed
delivered: head-nod approvals,
forced in, proteinaceous
meat-hams snoring
to shake awake in sub-
microscopic earthquakes and

yep, things
really start stirring now, things are
getting revved up; they sniff the air like
hounds: they align
this thing to that, a straight edge here,
tessellating there and finding

here we go, odd-bob molecules of
carbon dioxide drift aimlessly—here, grab
a hand or a shoulder, assign

firm purpose: intent: point:
objective, goal, thing to do, a mission not
impossible although energetically unlikely,
let me help you, first

take this, then do that, and
in mere milliseconds

reactions are roiling: constructing,
even as some things are torn down,
get remodeled, the net result
new walls, tile, a fresh paint job,

sugars, swelling, sweet me, honey,
I'm pure gold this morning

and the bees
by golly, dipping and bobbing the bold blue
spiderwort flowers,
they know it.

Learning through Travel

We flew from Knoxville to Dallas,
from Dallas to Los Angeles, and from there
to Papeet, French Polynesia—a long, long flight.

Where they first check the passports,
I bid the little pearl-handled pocketknife adieu,
all two inches of you: they tell me you need to ride
in checked luggage, folded to harmless sleep,
making new friends
with shorts and T-shirts.

Over the long flight we cannot sleep
even with a bulky neck pillow
snug beneath the chin: the thing
bulges in the wrong places.

For hours at a rate of more than 550
miles per hour, at an elevation similar to
38 thousand feet, the temperature is
minus 58 degrees Fahrenheit outside,
cold enough to freeze a monkey.

The first night there: the fan
in the bed-and-breakfast had three settings:
low, medium, and
extra-very-special high and
then it oscillated, sending
bubbly waves of air across
our bodies.

Breakfast later was good, then we sailed
out between small islands, snaking between
the red and green buoys: red,
danger from land, and green,
danger from reef.

Bounded to choppy sea. The empty place
is awash in numbers: 6
and a half knots, 137 degrees,
4-foot waves, off-scale

depth in meters,
a blue
blue blue deeper than you can imagine.

To reduce sea-sickness, we press
a scopolamine patch to the skin on the neck behind
the right ear: we sip ginger beer and stare hard
at Bora Bora on the horizon. We think
about reefs and the smooth water there.
For a while the blue plastic bucket,
its handle tied to a nylon rope, becomes
our good buddy, our best friend.

Towards Huahine, a member
of the Society Islands—a great expanse
of unruly waves and swells
breaks us from our minutia. An occasional

flying fish skims water for 50,
60, 70 meters before concussing
the side of a wave. The ocean,
after all, is
so empty, so blue.

For lunch we have deviled eggs,
a ham sandwich, sliced banana,
papaya, of course.

What does it take to learn a new place?
We learn all parts of a yacht should fit

organically to the whole: no hard edges
should come together firmly, none should attempt
to lock too tight with a twisted screw or a bolt. The joints

of the exoskeleton must have some give.
The sails, for example, want to accept
some flex; they want to accept
variation in pressure, some pull,
some heave and yaw. Yet still

we make more than 6 knots with slop
on slop, cross-
cutting hours of 3-foot waves.

The dingy
sports a 5-horsepower Mercury out-
board motor and contains two paddles
just in case. It is

inflated tight and snugged up
by winches at the back of the boat.
At night it is impossible
to get comfortable. The air
beneath deck is intensely humid and hot;

the tiny electric fan in the corner
above the bed pad makes noise but does not
appreciably move air; the two small hatches
through which we can peek do not
let in a cooling breeze without letting in
rain. Everything

keeps moving, moving.

Motoring
past islands into a lagoon, the water
becomes light blue, just 20 to 30 meters deep.
Coral heads, black fearsome under-
water lumps say, without

speaking, be very careful: inevitably

the yacht turns wide
into the wind, sails slip down. We learn
mooring, anchoring, docking.

The dingy gets a workout: perch on its sill,
water sprays to the faces
with intermittent waves.
Later, much later, too soon,
we say bye-bye, Bora Bora,
built up, a place we biked around
with a circumference of just 22 miles.

And later we say bye-bye
Tahiti, Raiatea, Tahaa, Huahine,
little islands in a big place,
less sand

than I had expected, more
coconut trees, pearls, and scooters.

Now, looking back, where
did we have that fantastic French-chef meal?
Whatever island it was, we took

the dingy to the dock, right at the restaurant's entrance:
tied it up, slipped on sandals,
went in, sat down and ate
such a meal! Bye-

bye, meal and hello
to sunburned arms, necks, backs of legs
despite being slathered
with reef-safe sunblock.

We snorkeled and watched
tiny blue fish boiling
from healthy protrusions of coral,
fist-sized yellow fish
with sharp black bars and snouty noses
cruising in and out of dark crevices,

and a small puffer fish that bowed up
and refused to puff, and so many
sea cucumbers and little things:
coral-embedded mollusks,
various snugged-in slick-shelled
bivalves and snails.

On one island we walked past
chickens and pigs, and we sweated
like pigs, going up and up
on switchbacks of a skinny road,

even past a herd of horses until
there we were, somehow, at the top,
a cell tower for company, with a small breeze
from the ocean since

the ocean was all around us and we could look down
over the lagoons, out to the reefs, all the way
to other islands, dark smudgy spots
on the horizon, and the road and a few cars

and scooters moving far below us.
There was our catamaran, moored
in the lagoon not too far from shore and
we drank deeply of water from bottles

in our daypacks, sweating it out
almost as fast as it went in, bye-
bye

Bora Bora, to your wild
Francs, about a penny each, it took
so many to buy even a mango—five thousand
for a bag of limes. All this to say, the ocean

was, for us, a new place: it touched us
as we learned.

Back to Edges

Again, I find myself
at the edges of things
I don't know—the pieces are rough
in some places and sharp

in others; some
have been recently broken; some
are so worn their fit is un-
certain. None of the pieces are labelled;
all of the pieces might, if placed properly,
make a beautiful whole thing

of indeterminate shape,
size and color, although
multi-color seems most likely and this

type of analysis
steers the wrong mind full steam
into the wrong-headed
business of probing and predicting.

Starting the Thing

Doofus cat buries herself
on the desk in shadow; she settles
promptly unlike me and
begins snoring. Sometimes she scratches
her jowls on the corner of the monitor,
    forcing it

off-kilter: cat-er-wampus. So many things
disrupt flow, add burbles, curlicues, off-
center adjustments of mass or velocity;
ovoids, not spheres, off-sets; things bend
toward lower energy: how much
is the question—
bending, I mean: should one, for example, genuflect

on one knee or on two, or go prone
with rump up, or flat out, in
maximum state of appeasement? Toes,
knees, belly, and chin to ground
if that might help, although I know of no
righteous reason why it might be so, unless

the party to be appeased appreciates
proneness in particular. Perhaps
that position is less threatening: it is
used by other animals expressing sub-
servience to their ilk: roll over, go

belly up, expose the throat, sing
hallelujah.

In the Shade

When I stepped back in time to hug
the young me, standing
forlorn in the shade
of the silver maple in the side yard

he hugged me back
thank God
and I told him then
without speaking I would be there

for him
through time. Now I can visit him
whenever he needs me,
there, in the shade.

I Lost It, Archie

He typed in strips while I wend
words, bending them to fit
the thought or sometimes curling
the thought to fit the words, and

occasionally whereas
and amongst the heretofores he broke
outright to a thing that caught
his eye or linked to something

inside that caught a thought
unattached to some other thought:
Lordy, one could dance a jig
or do the jitterbug just trying to

keep the thing alive. Not long
ago (ago), that is, just a short time
in the past, the wife and I were out
in lawn chairs on the deck overlooking

the koi pond and the water was
splashing and trickling beautifully
down the little waterfall,
and the koi were cruising about

like colorful submarines,
looking up for dinner, whereas and heretofore
we sipped our drinks
as the koi slurped stuff off the water surface

while waiting for their big manna to fall near dusk
amongst the lily pads where frogs huddled,
poking google eyes up from below the waterline.

One can reasonably ask where
the hell is this thing going? Or has it gone
already off the rails, irrevocably this time,

maybe down a ravine or worse
into a stony river, the bridge
    over which
we ride now, chatting sometimes and

singing hallelujah while people
we're passing stand wagging
bright parasols and noshing
popcorn as we

(the inverse of another
roadside attraction)

ride by, a choo-choo chug
feeling to the whole thing, a labored
lurching progress, and I,
yep, I'm still here, still

trying to capture the damned thing,
like he could and I can't:
more like a hobo just hanging on, hunched
in a dark corner of a boxcar.

Peeper Frogs in Early March

My running buddy Gus once said
it is that time of year again—
the peeper frogs are freezing
their little asses off.

This morning,
still dark, before six, I'm out
in the back yard, the dog
on a leash to keep her

from running full speed through the mud.
So far it has been
a dreadful start to spring—so much
rain, then more rain, day

after day, the back yard
is flooded and our lower-forty neighbor
has a new pond; it glints
under the slanty moon

and the peeper frogs, bless them
and their small hopes,
are creaking away, singing alleluia,
a chorus, despite the chill.

Screaming in a Dream

Last night I dreamed of the long-gone dad and
he was prattling on and on
about some useless thing while I
wanted so much to be heard: I kept

asking him, louder and louder, finally
screaming in a rage,
Are you going to listen to me?
Yes or no? Yes or no?

But he kept prattling, he was not
listening.

Some Things Pretend

You know, I could become a con-
trarian: fetch water when they say bring fire,
look for mushrooms when they say
find acorns. The way life is, we're damned

in any case: things seem con-
flated, con-
fused, con-
voluted, I am con-

cerned about where we're headed in this wimpy
day and age—actions keep crowding in,
nestling up, snuggling
as if they fit

even when they don't and

that's just half
the problem, the other half is
I'm not ex-
traordinary.

Some half things pretend
to be the other half. Once
on a motorcycle humming

due west on empty road in northern Arizona,
not far from New Mexico, the day
whipping by, I felt
free. And that feeling

doesn't
happen
often.

Stasis

I tried writing this morning but kept wanting
to get up and walk away: it is difficult
to get the brain to connect
the right pieces: it is difficult

to connect thoughts to place
where other thoughts live; it is difficult
to pull fear and taste it,
or caress wonder and push it.

I consider the road that bends
like a dream before me now; it is lined
with great trees casting shadows across it:
sunbeams dapple parts of the road

when the leaves near the tops of trees
bend a little this way or that way
under the slightest breeze, seemingly at play,
whimsically it seems,

but truth is they are certain
of their leverage: the trees are tall
so even small breezes
touching the top branches cause

motion, wanted or not, and there it is—
causality: the inevitable link
at the junction of still and move. The air
moves across the surface of a leaf, across

the surfaces of many leaves,
disrupting stasis, even molecules
of oxygen, nitrogen, carbon dioxide
move on their own accord while I

find myself hesitating, afraid, halfway
through step one. Three-
quarters of my life are behind me.

What's Left

After the bonfires of grief
have cleansed
as much as they can
there's still residue—

ashes and the last stale hint
of smoke in the air,
but oh, the beautiful
light released,

singing its silent way to the stars.

The Last

It has been said each first-born male
should be designated as holy, yet I ask
can we make holy

the last-born, too? Perhaps by offering
the lowest sacrifice—
a pair of turtle doves, or two young pigeons.

Now there are so many
that will be among the last—the last
of their kind: Martha, the last

passenger pigeon went out with palsy in 1914.
Lonesome George, the last Galapagos Tortoise
on Pinta Island, died in 2014.

Sudan, the last male northern white rhinoceros
died in 2018.
It won't be long now

before we see the last
mountain gorilla,
the last

vaquita, the last
hairy-nosed wombat, the last
elephant shrew, the last

Yangtze finless porpoise,
the last Amur leopard,
the last black-spotted cuscus,

the last
Hispaniolan solenodon.

PART 2

Strange Light

On the special day we went out early,
to see the eclipse, to be with friends, and we ate
hot dogs, and chips and watermelon, a few things
like that before driving the truck to the upper end
of the pasture, along the tree-encrusted edge
where we could hang out
in shade while the sun was still there,
and the wife and her boys and her ex
chatted loudly and laughed and got busy

setting up cameras
with special lenses on tripods
and I, of course, tested the pinhole thing
made from cardboard and aluminum foil,
and it worked fine, but things

in the cluster became too loud for me: I just wanted
to soak it all in—the soft

noises of the birds, the insects, the far-off
stamp of a horse hoof in the barn,
the small breeze rising, the slow hill
beginning to stir, a degree or two cooler
now from beneath the trees, several butterflies
bobbling more or less south, along the edge of
fresh-mowed pasture grass.
I just wanted

to take it all in; I just wanted

to feel the slow before;
I just wanted to anticipate
in quiet the abrupt rare moment as the light
lessened and grew strange.

A Slug While Hiking in Basque Country

In this place, a rock
is nothing like a stone.

As we walked, we took turns
leading, or following,

together sometimes, and sometimes
one ahead, leaving

prattle and a village behind,
and beyond a wall

of wild roses, blackberry bushes,
thistles, and ferns

a pasture, within which
a cowbell clanked softly,

and within which
fluttered a few small birds, like magpies

    but then

on rain-wet stones at the edge of the path,
creeping at

    oh, I don't know, a rate
    of several

millimeters per minute—
a glistening coal-black 5-inch slug.

We were out of place, of course, but
wherever he was, was home.

Ambition

I saw it first
in a young man's face: he was managing
the oil change for my truck.
I saw it in his eyes, his nose, and the cut
of his chin, the cheeks
shaved and pink and just past
pimple phase. He was occupied
not with oil change; rather, he was working
to slither up

the business food-web; he was focused
on rising: a low-level
manager today, become the boss
tomorrow, become the owner
later. Everything he did
and how he did it had that

objective. Later I saw
how others do it, too: they
relish the task. No action
is too small to count. They watch
for the smallest crack or flaw, the smallest
break or chink and

hook
something of themselves—like the tail-facing edge
of a snake's belly scale, or a lizard's claw, and
up they go, by raw force
or will or guile: a millimeter or two,
a centimeter on a good day,
that's the day

he goes home late, after work, gives
the wife a firm hug, tells her, it's
OK, hon, we're going to make it.

Waiting for Inspiration

So many little displacement
activities—take off

the glasses, wipe smears
off the lenses, pause to pick up

the coffee cup and slurp a slurp
while it's still hot; check

the monitor's settings, just to make sure
view is set at a percentage

I like, then take a quick look
or two out the window: white

tumbles of oak-leaf hydrangea
and dainty down-tipped leaves

of the dogwood, now past bloom;
and the yellow crooked-neck squash

plants in the raised-bed garden have not
grown at all—they seem positively stumped

about life and how to do it. This

morning, I went to church
to open doors and let in

the floor-refinishing crew—two rough guys
are going at it with big sanding tools;

they're taller and younger than I am; one
has a dandy set of tattoos down his left

muscled-up arm: the wood-dust
even with a vacuum is impressive. They steer

the noisy machines slowly the length of the floor.
The five-inch pine boards

shuck old dark surface stain, revealing
pallid gold beneath. And all this

is just a busy prelude
for living.

Two dogs tussle with a toy in the next room—
that's living, for them. For me,

it's a second swig of coffee. Archie said,
just start: it gets you to the plate: with

all the strikeouts, you may learn
to hit the ball.

So bottoms up to the cup. Hang
in there, Bud, something good

might happen.

By Satellite and Magazine

High over the southeast Atlantic Ocean,
moving 8 to 12 meters per second,
off the southwest coast of Africa,
thousands of square miles of thin clouds
block and bounce back
sunlight streaming towards the ocean below.

    But then

abruptly these clouds change: they clear
in several minutes, letting
sunlight through and this
massive clearing happens due to

    (WTF?)

fast-moving cloud-eroding atmospheric gravity waves
originating, likely, from western equatorial Africa.
Now wow! How neat is that?

My finger moves down the page,
learning.

Teaching a Science-Writing Workshop

I enter the building and rise
one floor by elevator—
smooth so far, coffee
cup in hand, the coffee

surface is one secure
centimeter below the rim and I think
whipped cream, now that would
really stabilize the liquid's surface,

reduce the risk of slop but
I'm happy, too, so far there is no slop: and thus
no honest need
for whipped cream. The cup-free hand

becomes engaged with handouts
of examples, copies of
a one-pager on the paramedic method,
a one-pager on useful scientific metaphors; you can look it up
on google dot com.

Eighteen interns assemble
in the boxy room, glancing at
the first PowerPoint slide: it seems

bigger now than it was
earlier this morning. They eye
my cup, the contents
still steaming. They pick up
the handouts and sign
the log sheet with
slashes and swirly scrawls.

They settle quietly into chairs around the table.

With the Margarita Half Gone

I wonder how matter works, and I think about
the nature of time—contemplate how things
at the quantum level jostle, settle in, and
    click

to one state or another—or so it seems
to us with our puny senses
and pathetic logic. In multiple
dimensions, the truth of some things

must be felt with the heart. Not all
can be made real by reason.

Fukushima Boars

First I imagine the damned things
bristled, broad shouldered,
snuffling and slobbering, curved tusks
glowing, dimly phosphorescent
in dark: when they attack, they bite
savagely, lunging forward, twisting
flesh in their jaws, slashing
as they turn to make sure
at least one tusk penetrates and rips
delicate flesh to bone. Then facts:

the wild boars are on a rampage;
they go in packs; they have muscled up.
Wild boar meat is a delicacy in Japan, but these animals
are too contaminated to eat—
some are hundreds of times
over the limit with radioactive Cesium.

Hunters take them down with traps and rifles,
drag them with machines, and bury them
in big holes gouged in the ground.

This Is for All the Forgetting

Yes, this poem is for that.
The forgetting, by a child,
of evil things, fears festering
from dark places next to the bed;
and later the forgetting
of crass actions, unthoughtful deeds,
things done that hurt
others to the quick; the forgetting

by teenagers, just mouthing around:
tongues of slander, spite, ridicule
and distain. The forgetting
of youth by encroaching age, and although
the brain knows not to do it, it does it
anyway. The sly innuendo, the half-
assed clever response, making the turn
you know you should not make.

The forgetting
of beauty by age; the forgetting
of each petal, each
wonderful blade of grass, each lovely thing
on Earth and beyond, as we give
what we have left.

Learning to Fly

Mathematical models have shown
most early birds, or reptiles like birds,
could not fly. Rather, they experimented

with feathers of various shapes,
and with big or small tails,
and with big or small wings, blundering
in evolutionary space with different

combinations of these things, mixed in with
combinations of gliding and flapping and
probably fast-running behaviors until

    jackpot! They got lucky.

Perhaps
it happened after they took a break:
they gossiped and considered

the collection of lift-
producing muscular efforts
needed to flap, and lungs plus air sacs,
a small body size, and

load lightening, accomplished
by shucking teeth
and using hollow bones.

Timing Is Everything

It is going to rain, perhaps
this afternoon, probably tonight, surely
sometime this week and two guys
are coming now with their black soup
and pressure spray tool, they're on their way,

this morning: it is 8:25 a.m. to be exact,
and the air is full-up heavy, muggy, mushed up
with humidity and overcast, the proverbial pause
before the storm, so should
we do this thing today, or not?
A week ago we tried to do it and
it rained hard before the job was half done
and the black crap

came down the asphalt drive, sliding evil rainbows,
saying, almost out loud,
gotcha, buddy, haha, gotcha good. The rain
rinsed it off before it had chance
to settle in, tidy up, dry out, hang tight.
A mess resulted, and after the rain

I had to scrub some sidewalk tiles hard
with a gasoline-soaked rag and hose things down
with detergent, and still the sealant
lurked in crevices, stinking
like tar and for days

we had a little La Brea Tar Pit
at the sidewalk's edge
and it even snagged a few
wandering ants and bugs.

Structure

The task of breaking things down to five-
line sets is problematic: the more natural
condition for me is quatrains, but bas-
tardized because a thought

started in one set does not finish there: rather

it carries over, and often spills over
again, through multiple sets. Four lines
just feels better sometimes and many times

I'll go back and bust the thing
to four-line sets. Archie did that

all over the map, some four, some five, some

with no breaks and no brakes,
he just let them big-eyed puppies steam

out of the station, mixing
a metaphor or two right there,
cold spring day, no clouds, bright sun.

The Rough Side of Spring

A hard bird-knock
to the window, a stunned fall of feathers,
a quick greasy smear—
yet it all turns out OK, I guess: she rises

before long, befuddled a bit, makes it
safe to a dogwood limb, the gray thing (bird)
holding tight to the gray thing (branch)
that holds tight a clutch of gnarly knobs of tight-
fisted terminal buds. They'll break

not too far into the future,
even though snow is predicted
two days hence, and meanwhile
the calico cat was, for an instant,
positively catatonic with excitement
when the bird bashed but

she has settled down now, too. It's all

working towards an agreement—a mistake
was made, the error
was corrected best it could be, likely a knot
on the head, probably not
bad as a cracked beak, unlikely
a lesson well learned: the glass is
transparent.

Oh, the robins get so fired up
this time of year! They ignore

crocuses, hyacinths, even the
skinny efforts of the *Forsythia*.
It flowers before it puts out leaves,
leaving it scraggly by nature in spring,
a hum-drum yellow against such
small herculean efforts of new green grass.

Demise of the Waggle Dance

Recent experiments show bees' waggle dances
are losing importance.
Compared to bees using the waggle dance,
bees in colonies with no dance language
make foraging flights averaging
eight minutes longer, and these flights yield

29 percent more nectar. What clever experiments
to learn such detailed things! The investigators
distract dancing bees by turning lights out
on the dance floor—no lasers, no music,

no disco ball. And, they upset the bees'
sense of spatial orientation, too,
by turning honeycombs
horizontally.

These new data now lead to suspicion: perhaps
humans have created foraging environments for which
the waggle-dance language is no longer well adapted.
Perhaps

the bees are busy converting
to American Sign Language, or
Esperanto, or to fine-scale
hieroglyphics,

written in honey, adorned with pollen.

On Making a Tuna Salad Sandwich
(with apology to William Carlos Williams)

From a physics book I recollect
the wobbles of Mercury
were by one man, in one blow, solved: the amount
of the procession of the perihelion of that

dinky planet, hot enough
to cook lead to vapor as I,

rendered inept with such a
poorly engineered mechanical device,
work hard to pop off
the lid from a tin can:
a tuna somewhere
outside my orbit must be

laughing bubbles as I crank

the thing, round
and around, a circular path with-
out much progress, without

satisfactory perihelion, converging
creep-wise at last to some success.

Yet cheesy questions still abound. Can I

open the mayonnaise jar or squeeze
a right-sized dollop of spicy mustard or safely dice
dill pickles with a knife? This is just to say

I think I'd almost rather eat

some plums
     from the icebox:
so easy, cold, and sweet.

Blank Page

I stare first at the blank page, then out the window
where drops of water hang
from the down-pointing
tips of dogwood leaves, bending
blades of grass, delicate tips

of totality. It seems
everything is wet and on the move from one place
to another. Global warming has caused
the hydrological cycle to speed up.
Now water moves

faster from the oceans to the air
and comes down harder and more sporadically
here and there with a vengeance,

but oddly the soil is drying faster now, too—
so dry places are getting drier, wet places
are getting wetter and here

I am, doing nothing, just
writing and staring.

A Small Hibernaculum, Revisited

1 ■
    Working now with the word
    hibernaculum: a place, a winter refuge,
    where a creature chooses to hibernate;
        it could be
    a cave, a cavity in a tree, a rocky den,
    a dead-leaf wad in a hole in the ground, or a shelter for
        toads
        bats
        rattlesnakes
        insects
        bears, of course,
        skunks
        bees
        chipmunks
    and there's a strange fine line between
    hibernation and torpor,
    perhaps just a matter of degree.

2 ■
    A staying change: a re-
    peating motion, en-
    capsulated in reason although reason is
    no better than ambience, according to

    Archie Ammons—his poem
    "Hibernaculum" snugs up
    one thousand and eight lines dispersed
    evenly in one hundred and twelve stanzas
    mostly to say—beautifully I must add,

a lot of what
   just
      makes
         sense.

and in there: a breakdown of

        car-repair costs, snow squalls,
        a task of putting up a tent
        (in a basement, no less)
        a hibernaculum
        inside a hibernaculum, and

in multiple ways the plural thereof,
of various sorts, and note here
unlike Archie, I did not even try to break things out
in three-line groups, three groups
per stanza.

No Hallelujahs

Here's a list
of things that affect or relate
to the place where you live—to your zip
code, your home:

>   Risk of breaking a bone
>   Risk of cardiac arrest
>   The robustness of your immune system
>   Your life expectancy
>   Your size, small or large—if you're a turtle.
>   Your access to legal aid
>   Likelihood of dying from cancer
>   Rates of marijuana use
>   Severity and prevalence of cataracts
>   Your education and religion

Where you live is such a significant
predictor of health, and unstable housing is
associated with health complications, including

>   asthma
>   depression
>   exposure to lead and other
>   toxic elements.

What a mess. If you hang out
sometimes at the water cooler, chances are
you may live longer. And speaking of

      homeless
   and hanging out and
      exposure to this and that
I discovered

Anolis porcatus, a plucky little lizard—
so persistent and resolute! He worked his way up
by his bootstraps; he worked his way up
starting with nothing

in Cuba, from zip 33300—and he made it
somehow to Brazil and
succeeded: now he's a new pest in a new home.

I Feel So Earthy and Down at Home

Archie whined a lot
but he put things straight: no
messing around with this or that, in *Glare*

for example he just comes out and says
the thing—strip or no strip, tight like
the boats' reflections too

glassy to bob, the ducks flicking,
drawing those huge wedges of
ripples behind them, and meanwhile I,

near puttered out in Pie Town, have
achy feet and tired fingers; work hard
pruning this and that, sometimes

even taking a saw
to a larger thing, or applying
loppers to some pathetic leafy thing, stinky

as a wet hound in August, ears
flopped down, nose up, mud to knees.
I must remember he said this: company

chitchat keeps chitchat cheap—
and there's the rub with *Glare*.

Not Today, It Doesn't

My desk is half-
way to chaos and it is
aggravating but it works
sometimes: *Science*
magazines in a sloppy pile, poetry
books in stacks, one
open, most closed: think,
I think, of an analogy for that.

And the open book of course is *Glare*:

it just keeps circling back. Let the it's
in this case be ambiguous—
make it what you'd have it be.
So the right thing is

pause, look out the window: trees
of several kinds, things are flying
towards summer now, a pole
with a transformer sup-
porting multiple wires, four at least
running to this house and some
electrician had fun with that I bet and

above and well beyond that, cloudy
notions, a possibility of rain. I learned
today, we (the US of A) have (or has)
soldiers in 80 countries where
fighting is going on, so those chaps
and gals

come under fire sometimes and
bullets don't have friends.

When time runs out, these guys
(and gals) just
end their tours, one

way or another: they get off
the team, go home, wrapped
up or not, they don't

get off because the war ends,
because it doesn't

end.

Not the Same

The moon has circled me now
eight hundred forty-three times

or more: that's
a lot of circling, so surely

some night, I think, it will settle down,
hone in on

that which emanates from me,
like pale blue light,

Cherenkov radiation:
like that which emanates from me,

silent as gamma rays from my core,
or that which foams like

spooky action at a distance. With so much
circling, I have grown confident

uncertainty is not the same
as ambiguity.

About the Author

Arthur J. Stewart's poems have been published in more than a dozen national and regional poetry anthologies and in various literary and scientific magazines, including *Rattle, Journal of the American Medical Association, Lullwater Review, Big Muddy, New Millennium Writings, Bulletin of the Ecological Society of America,* and *Chemical & Engineering News.* He was a 1997 Tennessee Poetry Prize winner, a 2009 winner of the Wilma Dykeman Prize for essay writing, and a 2013 inductee into the East Tennessee Writers Hall of Fame for poetry. He served as writer-in-residence at Michigan State University's Kellogg Biological Station and has given science writing workshops for undergraduate, graduate, and postgraduate science interns at U.S. Department of Energy facilities in Tennessee, West Virginia, Pennsylvania, South Carolina, Oregon, and Colorado. *The Hallelujah Series* is his seventh collection of poems.

www.ingramcontent.com/pod-product-compliance
Lightning Source LLC
Chambersburg PA
CBHW031210090426
42736CB00009B/859